# THE NATURE AND DEVELOPMENT

## OF T

### 1.

The Thai language as spoken by the people of
Thailand is, in its original structure, to a certain extent
comparable with Chinese. Hence the two languages, i.e.
the Thai and the Chinese, are philologically grouped together into the same family of languages. There are in both
of these languages a number of similar words running to
many hundreds. No doubt these words are in most cases
due to cultural borrowings after long and continual contact
of the two peoples historically in the old days both in
peace and war. Nevertheless, there are certain classes of
words which apparently might have come from a common
source in remote times.

**The Word.** Fundamentally the Thai language in
monosyllabic in its formation of words. It is a charac-
teristic to be found also in Chinese and, more or less, in
other language groups of South - East Asia. Due to the
limited number of combinations of sounds which the consonants admit, there arises naturally a multitude of words
with the same sound but with a difference in meaning
(=homonyms). With such a phenomenon the Thai language
has availed itself of the use of tones as a primary feature
of the language to differentiate meaning in homonymous
words. Each word is complete in itself and admits no
modifications as do the inflectional languages with their
differences of case, gender, number, etc. There is no hard

and fast rule that makes Thai words belong to a particular part of speech. Any word may become a noun, a verb, an adjective or an adverb, etc., simply through the position of the word in the sentence. Each word stands distinctly and independently, and concedes no joining of sounds or assimilations between words. (There are five tones in the standard Thai language, but in actual speaking there may be six or even seven tones varying in certain dialectical areas. )

Even though differentiation of words by tones has been introduced into the system, there is still a considerable number of homonymous words. Unless the context of a phrase or a sentence shows otherwise, the meaning of the word may still be ambiguous. In such instances, some other word or words have to be introduced to clarify the meaning. There are three devices for doing this, viz.

1. By prefixing a meaningful word to indicate the class of objects to which the word belongs.

For example: "Yang" ( ยาง ) may mean *a bird* such as heron, egret or bittern; *a tree* such as a *dipterocarpeaeii*, rubber tree; *an oily and sticky substance* such as resin, gum, latex, wood oil. If the word "nok" ( นก ) meaning *bird* is prefixed it becomes "nok yang" (นกยาง) which means either *a heron, an egret* or *a bittern*. If the word "ton" ( ต้น ) meaning *a bole* or *a trunk of a tree* is prefixed to the word "yang" in "ton yang" ( ต้นยาง ) it means a species of trees *(Dipterocarpus alatus)*.

We may call such prefixed words *Classifiers*.

2. By juxtaposing two meaningful words of the same or allied meaning to clarify a certain word:

For example : " Kha fan " (ฆ่าฟัน ) means *to kill*. The word " kha " has a number of meanings, and one of them is *to kill*. If the word is juxtaposed together with the word " fan " meaning *to slash with a weapon*. The word cannot mean otherwise than to kill only. The word "fan", as juxtaposed, serves to clarify the meaning of the word " kha ". Some juxtaposed words have sometimes lost their individual independent meanings in current use and have become merely a juxtaposing word only.

Sometimes two words of the same or allied meaning are juxtaposed to form a new meaning of an allied kind.

For example: " Ban müang " (บ้านเมือง) means *country, nation* ( ban = *village*, müang = *city or town* ).

Sometimes four words are joined together to form a phrase but with a single meaning.

For example : " Khao yak mak phaeng " ( ข้าวยากหมาก แพง ) means *famine*. ( khao = *rice*, yak = *scarce*, mak = *fruit*, phaeng = *dear* ).

In forming such words or phrases there is an unconscious selection of sounds. A word with a prominent or more musical sound is selected always as a second of the two words. In the joining of four words in the form of a phrase as cited above the two words between the first and last word are mostly rhymed.

The juxtaposed words as described may be called *synonymous compounds*.

3. By joining into a compound a simple verb to which is added the object logically inherent in it.

For example: "ying pün" (ยิงปืน) literally "fire gun" = to shoot, "kin toh" (กินโต๊ะ) literally "eat (on) table" = *to dine on a table*. "Non sua" (นอนเสื่อ) literally "sleep (on a) mat".

One is apt to recognize such compound words as one factor that makes pidgin English. Karlgren in his book "Sound and symbols in Chinese" gives such compound words in the Chinese also. He calls them *Elucidative Compounds.*

Thai, like the Chinese and other languages of South-East Asia, uses enumerative words when using numbers with nouns. There are a large number of this category of words for each appropriate noun.

If in some nouns no numeral descriptive noun can be appropriately used, or one cannot remember if there is such an appropriate one, the noun is repeated after the number.

For example: "Khon si khon" (คนสี่คน) i.e. "man, four men". "Ma sam ma" (ม้าสามม้า) i.e. "horse, three horses". In this instance the appropriate numeral descriptive word is "tua" (ตัว) which will be "Ma sam tua" (ม้าสามตัว) i.e. "horses three bodies", but the former phrase "ma sam ma" can be tolerated as Thai also.

There is a tendency for Thai monosyllabic words to become dis-syllabic ones similar to those of Malay, but they differ fundamentally from Malay in that the Thai dis-syllabic words are mostly of euphonic couplets only.

Stone Inscription of King Ram Khamhaeng. vide p. 22

King Ram Khamhaeng's Inscription in details.

There are many ways of creating such words. A few examples may suffice.

1. By variation of the vocalic sound in a word with vowels adjoining in articulation sequence.

For example: "Non" (นอน) meaning *sleep* has "naen" (แนน) or "noen" (เนิน) as its couplet. The second word or syllable has no recognized meaning in the language; an omission of it would leave the meaning intact. There are a large number of this kind of dissyllabic words unconsciously uttered by speakers mostly in colloquial use. These euphonic words or endings are sometimes to be found as actual words in certain dialects and also in some of the Thai languages outside Thailand. In fact some of these euphonic words remind us equally of certain Chinese words as compared with Thai ones.

For example: "Ngo" (โง่) means stupid in Thai and has "ngau" (เง่า) as its euphonic ending. In the Chinese Cantonese dialect a stupid or a dull fellow is "ngau". Among the Chinese dialects there is the same tendency to vowel mutation. Tooth in Cantonese dialect is "nga", but become "nge" in Swatow dialect. "Nga" is identical with the Thai "nga" (งา) meaning tusk, ivory.

2. By varying the vowel of a word with its corresponding, but not necessarily adjoining vowel sound. Such vowel sounds are "aw - ae (ออ - แอ), o - e (โอ-เอ), u - i (อุ - อี)

For example: "Ngawn - ngan" (ง่อนแง่น) = *infirm, unstable*; "tong - teng" (โตงเตง) = *to sway to and fro in a dangling position*; "Chu - chi" (ชุ่ชี่) = *peevish, fretful.*

A word with a vowel-diphthong may also have a coresponding diphthong as its euphonic ending.

For example: "Yua-yia" (ยั้วเยี้ย) = *swarming:* "mau-mai" (เมามาย) = *intoxicated.*

A great number of this class of euphonic endings are mostly onomapoetic words, and with a few exceptions, neither the first word nor its second word or ending can be divorced from its combination without losing its particular meaning.

3. By changing words ending in unexplosive consonants *k, t, p* into their corresponding nasal endings *ng, n, m* respectively.

For example: "Saek-saeng" (แทรกแซง) = *intervene, interfere,* "Saek" alone means *insert, squeeze in,* while "saeng" means *interpose, insert.*

"Thot-thon" (ถอดถอน) = *remove.* "Thot" means *take off* as a garment, *dismiss, discharge* while "thon" means *pull out, root out.*

"Yap-yam" (หยาบหยาม) = *contemptuous, insult.* "Yap" means *crude, rough* while "yam" means *revile, look down on.*

Each word in the couplet as cited above has a slight shade of meaning if used independently. Sometimes there is a change, the word ending in a nasal taking on an open vocalic ending.

For example: "thon-thoi" (ถอนถอย) Thoi= *to withdraw.* Thus we have a set of three differer words "thot, thon, thoi" (ถอด, ถอน, ถอย) with a slight difference of sound and meaning to each of the words in the set.

To sum up there are many types of these dissyllabic words. The above three types are quoted as certain examples only, and there are numerous others mostly in colloquial use. There is no difficulty in commanding such dis-syllabic words, for they will come unconsciously to the speakers. Many of these words have become everyday speech of the people. Foreigners who can speak Thai and command such words in their daily speech are admired by the native speakers of the language as people who speak Thai like a Thai.

As the Thai language has no method of forming new words by means of additions to a word like the inflectional languages with their affixes and case endings, the various processes described above are evidently devices by which the Thai have formed derivatives and new words.

**The Sentence.** The arrangement of words in a sentence in the Thai language is fundamentally "Subject-action-object," with qualifying words, adjectives and adverbs, which, as in most of the languages of South-East Asia, follow each appropriate word. There is no hard and fast rule relating to "parts of speech" in the actual sense of the word. A word may be noun, adjective, verb, or adverb only in relation to other words in a phrase or a sentence. Hence the important thing in the Thai language is the word order. "Grammatical words", such as articles, prepositions, conjunctions, etc. which serve as a help to clarify the "real words", i.e. nouns, verbs, etc. in a sentence, are not necessary if the context in the sentence is logically clear.

For example: If we want to say "a father and a son sit on chairs", this will be in Thai "father child sit chair". ( พ่อลูกนั่งเก้าอี้ )

As many words of the same part of speech may be strung together as desired, provided each word be in its logical position or sequence of time in the case of verbs.

For example: If we want to say "a big black dog chases a small white cat and bites it", in Thai this will be "dog black body big run chase bite cat white body small". ( หมาดำตัวโตวิ่งไล่กัดแมวขาวตัวเล็ก )

Frequently two or more words are combined to express one notion, when the second and subsequent members stand in adjectival relationship to the first.

For example: "Fai fa" ( ไฟฟ้า ) means literally "fire-sky" (i.e. *sky* - fire ) = electricity. "Mai kheet fai" ( ไม้ขีดไฟ ) means literally *stick - strikes - fire* = a match or matches.

As already stated the Thai words admit no modifications respecting differences of case, number and gender.

For example: "Khon ma ha khao" ( คนมาหาเขา ) may mean *a man* ( or men, woman, women ) *comes* ( or come, coming, came, has come, etc.) *to see him* ( or he, she, it, they, them ). If the meaning is not clear in the mind of the hearer then "grammatical words", or "help words" as the Chinese call them, are introduced into the sentence.

For example: "Khon song khon cha ma ha khao" (คนสองคนจะมาหาเขา) literally means *man two men will come see him*. The word "Khon" in this case is <u>men</u>, and the word "khao" is <u>him</u> or <u>them</u> etc.

It will be seen that Thai "words are symbols of concept *per se*, being wholly devoid of inflectional apparatus to express and define their relations with other words in the sentence. They are, therefore, free to function in any syntactical relation not incompatible with their essential meaning". (*Some Features of the Siamese Speech and Writing* by Cornelius B. Bradley, J. R. A. S. 1923, Century Supplement).

Students of the Chinese language will readily recognize a close similarity in the construction of word and sentence between Chinese and Thai. Perhaps due to a long standing intercourse between the Thai and the Chinese, the two languages, if not akin, have acquired a tendency to affinity in character.

The Thai language has one of the simplest grammars of all languages as far as inflections are concerned. It is not tied by rules and conventions. But in the course of its historical and cultural development, the Thai language has suffered at the hands of Thai grammarians, through exotic rules and restrictions based on English, Sanskrit or Pali grammar.

## 2.  The Development

Based upon somewhat scanty data of certain basic words and the linguistic formations of the languages of the many Thai minority groups to be found scattered here and there in the present day in Southern China and its adjacent lands, we may presume that the language of the Thai of Thailand is still similar in its fundamental aspects to that of the ancient languages of their ancestors.

In the course of history many groups of Thai speaking people, who also called themselves Thai *(or its unaspirated form " Tai " )* migrated into the Indo-Chinese Peninsula from their old home in Southern China in different groups and in different directions and periods of time.  We do not know for certain when and how the earlier migrations of these groups of people took place, but let us say with diffidence that these migrations happened some time not less than ten centuries ago.  One group of this people became the Shans in Upper Burma, another became the Thai of Thailand another became the Laos of the Lao Kingdom, not to speak of other minority groups with many local names to be found here and there in the Northern parts of the Indo-Chinese Peninsula.

Confining ourselves to one group in particular, the Thai of Thailand, we can say that they have mixed freely with the people of the Mon-Khmer linguistic group, therefore-runners, both ethnically and culturally.  By "Mon-Khmer" linguistic group here I mean the Mons and the Khmers in particular.  Through the close contact of the Thai with these peoples, firstly with the Mon-speaking race, akin perhaps to the Mons of Lower Burma, and secondly with the Khmers, the ancestors of the Cambodians, the Thai in Thailand have acquired a blending, predominantly in Central Thailand, making certain racial and cultural traits peculiarly their own. They were known thereafter and until recently as the Siamese. The Thai language of the Siamese had by this time seen a substantial change in vocabulary, by far the greatest influence being that of the Mon-Khmer languages.

Mon-Khmer languages in certain aspects are similar to Thai. Their basic words are largely monosyllabic and isolating in character with respect to word order, but unlike the Thai, they have prefixes and infixes to form their derivative words, while Thai had none in its original language system. The Mon-Khmer languages also admit certain initial consonantal clusters of two or more non-syllabic sounds to many of their words. Thai, on the other hand, apparently lacks such a feature in words as occurring in the various dialects, with the exception of the Siamese and the Ahom of Assam. Some scholars have maintained that old Thai had such features too, but has lost them at a later date. Anyhow, through the contact with Mon-Khmer, the Siamese language, especially in Central Thailand, has absorbed, to a great extent, these two features of the Mon-Khmer, i.e. the use of prefix and infix and initial consonantal clusters in words.

Central Thailand roughly in the 5th to the 13th century A.D. was within the political orbit of the Mons and the Khmers successively. The Mons at that time were a comparatively civilized race in the Indo-Chinese Peninsula. They had received their civilization from India and had adopted Buddhism; while the Khmers another civilized race of that period were a highly hindu-ized people. Consequently, the Mons and the Khmers had in their language a considerable number of words derived from the Pali and Sanskrit languages. As the Mon and Khmer languages are largely monosyllabic, loan words from Pali and Sanskrit are usually clipped and reduced, if possible, to a minimum monosyllabic form, and sounds are changed to meet the phonetic system peculiar to the language.

Although in time the Siamese became the paramount race in Central Thailand in succession to the Khmers, it is reasonable to suppose that the bulk of the population might still have been predominantly Mons and Khmers. These were gradually and naturally absorbed by the Thai and, as an important ingredient, became part and parcel of the race known as the Siamese. The Thai language had by now changed much through the influence of the Mon-Khmer. More and more Mon and Khmer words were adopted into the Thai language.

Moreover, words of Sanskrit and Pali origin were introduced into the Siamese language, at first through the medium of the Mon and the Khmer languages, and later through direct borrowing from India and Ceylon. Sanskrit and Pali are at the opposite pole from the Thai language. The former are grammatically inflectional

Stone Inscription of King Lu Thai,
14th century A.D.

Chiangmai Inscription at Wat Chiangman, 16th century A.D.
Based on Sukhothai script.

languages where words are bound by cases and other endings, while the latter is an analytic one with words that are independent and free in their grammatical form. Words from Sanskrit and Pali borrowed by the Thai do not, therefore, strictly adhere to the rules of inflections; such words become isolating when naturalized as Thai, and words of Sanskrit and Pali with many syllables are clipped and reduced, if possible, in the same manner as in the Mon and Khmer languages. Likewise Sanskrit and Pali sounds are changed naturally to conform with the Thai phonetic system.

Going back to the Mon and Khmer languages, we can say that the Thai, after their consolidation as a paramount race in Thailand, had gradually absorbed in their Thai language a fairly large number of Mon and Khmer words as revealed in their current use both in speaking and in Thai literature. In fact, the Thai had even adopted the device of making derivatives from their indigenous words with prefixes and infixes of the Mon-Khmer language. In a later period of history the situation was comparatively in reverse. Instead of the Thai borrowing words from the Mon-Khmer language, in particular the Khmer, the latter drew on a fairly large number of Thai words as part of their vocabulary. Paradoxically, many Thai words of Khmer origin were borrowed back by the Khmers unconsciously in new phonetic forms peculiar to the Thai pronunciation. The mutual borrowings of both languages are clear and discrete, for the borrowed words were fully naturalized in both of the two languages. At the present day an intelligent Thai, when reading Khmer writing in Thai transliteration, will be able to identify easily many words as identical with his ówn; not to speak also of words drawn from Sanskrit and Pali from which the two languages have borrowed abundantly. It is in speaking only that the two languages are mutually unintelligible because of different phonetic systems.

In adopting words of exotic origin into the Thai language, the Thai have made use of their old device of forming "synonymous couplets", probably to translate their newly adopted foreign words by juxtaposing them with the Thai indigenous ones which had similar meanings.

For instance: "Ton-doem" ( ต้นเดิม ) in Thai means *origin*. "Ton" is a Thai indigenous word meaning *bole, base*; while "doem" is Khmer in origin meaning *beginning* or *first cause*. "Thiang-trong" ( เที่ยงตรง ) means *upright, just,* "Thiang" is a Thai word meaning *correct, sure*; while "trong" is a Khmer word meaning *straight*. There are a large number of Thai words of this type. The same was done, also, to words of Indian origin.

For instance: "Sap-sin" ( ทรัพย์สิน ) means *asset*. "Sap" in "dravya" is Sanskrit meaning *wealth*, while "sin" is Thai meaning *money*. (compare Chinese) "t'sin" in Cantonese dialect - which means *money*. "Rup-rang" ( รูปร่าง ) means *feature, shape, form*. "Rup" is "rupa" in its Sanskrit and Pali form, while "rang" is Thai meaning *structural form*.

One feature of the Mon-Khmer language, as already mentioned, is the use of prefix and infix. An infix is an insertion of a sound into a radical or basic word to form a variation of meaning. Such a feature the Thai language did not originally have. Through the intimate contact of the Thai with the Khmer in the past, a large number of such words are to be found in the Thai language.

In Thai words taken from Khmer, for example, the word "truat" (ตรวจ) means *examine, inspect*. With a sound "am" (อำ) infixed into it, it becomes "tamruat" (ตำรวจ) and means *police, guard*, "Phak" (พัก) means *rest*. With "n" as an infix it becomes "phnak" (พนัก) meaning a *support* as for instance of a chair. With "am" as an infix it becomes "phamnak" (พำนัก) meaning a *support* (in time of distress or difficulty).

Sometimes the meaning of such Khmer infixed words, when introduced into the Thai language, does not change from that of the radical words. For example: "Charoen" (เจริญ) means *increase, prosper*, with "am" as an infix it becomes "chamroen" (จำเริญ) which has the same meaning as "charoen" in Thai, while in Khmer "Charoen" is a causative, *to make an increase* or *cause to prosper*.

In certain cases the Thai use such Khmer infixes to form their own words. For example; "Siang" (เสียง) in Thai means *noise, sound*. With an infix "amn" it becomes "Samniang" (สำเนียง) which means *voice, sound, timbre*, (compare the Chinese word, pronounced as "seng" in the Cantonese dialect, which means, *sound, voice, noise, speech.*)

In the Thai language there is a conventionalized set of words called "rachasap" (ราชาศัพท์) or court language. Certain basic words such as *eat, walk, sit, sleep, head, hands, hair, feet*, etc., have special words appropriate to the

### Consonants

| | k | kh | kh' | k' | k'' | kh' | ng | č | ch | c' | ç | ch' | y' | d |
|---|---|---|---|---|---|---|---|---|---|---|---|---|---|---|
| King Ram Kamhaeng, 1283 A.D. | | | | | | | | | | | | | | |
| King Lu Thai, 1357 A.D. (grandson of above) | | | | | | | | | | | | | | |
| Chiangmai Area, 1518 A.D. | | | | | | | | | | | | | | |
| Lao script. | | | | | | | | | | | | | | |
| King Narai, 1660 A.D. | | | | | | | | | | | | | | |
| Compressed Thai Characters. | | | | | | | | | | | | | | |
| Thai Writing, Tamarind-leaf shape. | | | | | | | | | | | | | | |
| Thai Writing, King Rama I (1782-1809) | | | | | | | | | | | | | | |

## VOWELS

| | ǫ | a | ï | i | ü' | u' | ·ü | u | ṛü' | ru' | ḷu | įu' | e | ae | |
|---|---|---|---|---|---|---|---|---|---|---|---|---|---|---|---|
| King Ram Kamhaeng, 1283 A.D. | | | | | | | | | | | | | | | |
| King Lu Thai, 1357 A.D. (grandson of above) | | | | | | | | | | | | | | | |
| Chiangmai Area, 1518 A.D. | | | | | | | | | | | | | | | |
| Lao script. | | | | | | | | | | | | | | | |
| King Narai, 1660 A.D. | | | | | | | | | | | | | | | |
| Compressed Thai Characters. | | | | | | | | | | | | | | | |
| Thai Writing, Tamarind-leaf shape | | | | | | | | | | | | | | | |
| Thai Writing, King Rama I (1782-1809) | | | | | | | | | | | | | | | |

# THAI ALPHABETS

## CONSONANTS

| ṇ | d | t | th | t' | th' | n | b | p | ph | f | p' | f' | ph' | m | y | r | l | w | s' | ṣ | s | h | ! | h' |
|---|---|---|----|----|-----|---|---|---|----|---|----|----|-----|---|---|---|---|---|----|----|----|----|----|----|
| ก | ด | ต | ถ | ท | ธ | น | บ | ป | ผ | ฝ | พ | ฟ | ภ | ม | ย | ร | ล | ว | ศ | ษ | ส | ห | ฬ | |
| ข | ด | ต | ฐ | ฑ | ฒ | ณ | บ | ป | ผ | ฝ | พ | ฟ | ภ | ม | ย | ร | ล | ว | | | ส | ฮ | | |
| ค | ด | ฑ | ฒ | ณ | ถ | ท | บ | ป | ฝ | | | | พ | | ม | ญ | ร | ล | ว | | ศ | ษ | ห | ฯ |
| ฅ | ด | ฏ | ฌ | | | ฒ | ณ | บ | ฎ | ฏ | ฐ | ฑ | ฒ | | ม | ญ | ร | ล | ฦ | | | ส | ห | | ร |
| ฆ | ด | ฑ | ฒ | ณ | ถ | ท | น | บ | ป | ผ | ฝ | พ | | ภ | ม | ย | ร | ล | ว | ศ | ษ | ส | ห | |
| ฉ | ฉ | ฌ | ฑ | ฒ | ณ | ด | ต | ถ | ท | ธ | น | บ | ป | ผ | ฝ | พ | ร | ล | ว | ศ | ษ | ส | ฬ | |
| ฒ | ด | ต | ก | ท | ร | น | บ | ป | ผ | ฝ | พ | ฟ | ภ | ม | ป | ร | ล | ว | ศ | ษ | ส | ห | ฬ | ฮ |
| | ด | ฑ | ณ | ฒ | น | บ | ป | ผ | ฝ | พ | ฟ | ฮ | ณ | ด | ร | | ล | ว | | | ส | ห | ฬ | ๏ |

## NUMERICAL FIGURES

| ăm | äh | | | | | | | | | | | 1 | 2 | 3 | 4 | 5 | 6 | 7 | 8 | 9 | 0 |
|----|----|---|---|---|---|---|---|---|---|---|---|---|---|---|---|---|---|---|---|---|---|
| +ำ | +ั | | | | | | | | | | | ๑ | ๒ | ๓ | ๔ | | ๕ | | | | |
| +ำ | +ั | | | | | | | | | | | ๑ | ๒ | | | | | ๗ | | ๙ | |
| +ิ | +ะ | | | | | | | | | | | ๒ | ๓ | ๕ | ๖ | ๗ | ๘ | ๗ | ๘ | ๙ | |
| +ู | +ะ | | | | | | | | | | | ๑ | ๒ | ๓ | ๔ | ๕ | ๖ | ๗ | ๘ | ๒ | ๐ |
| +ี | +ั | | | | | | | | | | | | | | | | | | | | |
| +ู | +ั | | | | | | | | | | | | | | | | | | | | |
| +ำ | +ั | | | | | | | | | | | | | | | | | | | | |
| +ั | ั | | | | | | | | | | | | | | | | | | | | |

king and princes. These words are in the main Khmer, Sanskrit and Pali in origin. The rest, a fair number, are Thai words which have been coined so as to differentiate them from the ordinary words. Khmer words belonging to the Thai court language are interesting ones, for they are common words of the Khmer language used currently. Perhaps in the old days when the Thai became a ruling race in Central Thailand displacing the Khmers, the Thai ruling class had probably been enculturised to a certain extent by Khmer culture. Hence certain Khmer words were elevated in meaning through the medium of the literature of that period, which mostly dealt with divine beings, kings and princes.

We now come to another language, the Malayo-Javanese, which played a not unimportant part in the development of words in the Thai language. Through the medium of this language, the Thai have received a fairly large number of foreign words of Semitic origin, namely, Arabic and Persian Arabic of later periods, and also of Portuguese origin.

Malayo-Javanese language groups, with the exception of their dis-syllabic words and the use of affixes, i.e. prefix, infix and suffix, agree substantially with the Thai and most other language groups in South-East Asia. We do not know how much their people, particularly the Malays, have mixed in blood and language with the people on the mainland of South-East Asia in ancient days, in particular, near the seacoast. In fact some scholars think that the Thai language bears a striking resemblance to Malayo-Javanese or Indonesian. They further state that there is an affinity existing between these two language groups. This may well be true to a certain extent, if it is true at all, where the two races have mixed to a considerable degree.

By comparing in a haphazard manner, there emerge a large number of Malay words common to Thai and other language groups of Thailand's neighbours. No doubt most of these words are due to cultural borrowings. In the 18th century A.D. the well known Javanese Panji Cycle Tales were introduced into the Thai language and became one of the popular romances in Thai literature ( *see* " Thai Literature in Relation to the Diffusion of Her Cultures " No. 9 *in this series* ). Through the introduction of these stories a fairly large number of Javanese words are to be found in the Thai language which are understood comparatively well by the Thai people, though most of such words are of a literary kind.

Like the Indonesian language group, the Thai language in a later period has adopted Chinese words, relating to names of certain articles and of food peculiar to the Chinese race, and a number of words in connection with trade and commerce. Most of these words are used colloquially, but many of them have also been naturalized fully into the Thai language. Chinese words in Thai are of the Tie-Chiu or Swatow dialect while in Malay they are of the Fukianese one. This is due to whichever speakers of either of these dialects are predominant in the land.

Last of all, and no less important in the development of the Thai language, is English. Though there are comparatively few English words to be found in Thai, the influence of expression in Thai both in speaking and writing among younger generations along the lines of English or American forms of sentence and idiom is seen more and more obviously through the medium of television, radio and translation.

### 3. The Thai Alphabet

The Thai alphabet is indirectly of Indian origin. In 1283 A.D., the great King Ram Khamhaeng of the Thai of the Sukhothai Dynasty of Thailand (*see* "Introducing Cultural Thailand in Outline", No. 1 *of this series*), instituted the present Thai alphabet. Though modelled on the Indian one through the medium of the old Khmer characters, the Thai alphabet differs from the Indian and the Khmer source in two essential points.

In Indian and Khmer writing when two or more consonants come in contact as an initial or an ending of a word or a syllable, they coalesce into one whole when written: a certain consonant *(or consonants)* becomes abbreviated in form when juxtaposed with the main one. Suppose the English word grasp is to be written in the Indian or Khmer style, the initial *gr* of the word grasp and also of *sp* of its ending will have to be coalesced as one whole by abbreviating the *r* and the *s* and blending them with their respective *g* and *p*. King Ram Khamhaeng split them each into independent characters, like the Roman alphabet, in the same manner as one writes the English word "grasp" above.

Thai handwriting, another type of compressed style—a facimile of
a letter from the Siamese officials to the Danish authority on a new
law on trade as promulgated by the Siamese Government, 1621 A.D.

อักษรไทยย่อ ครั้งสมเด็จพระนารายน์

หนังสือสัญญาระหว่างสยามประเทศกับประเทศฝรั่งเศส

พ.ศ. ๒๒๓๐

Thai handwriting, compressed style—a facimile of a treaty of friendship and commerce between Siam and France, 1687 A.D.

# MODERN THAI ALPHABET
**WRITTEN SCRIPT, ELABORATE STYLE.**

---

ก ข ฃ ค ฅ ฆ ง

จ ฉ ช ซ ฌ ญ

ฏ ฐ ฑ ฒ ณ

ด ต ถ ท ธ น

บ ป ผ ฝ พ ฟ ภ ม

ย ร ล ว ศ ษ ส ห ฬ อ ฮ

อะ อา อำ อิ อี อึ อื อุ อู เอะ เอ

แอะ แอ โอะ โอ เอาะ ออ เออะ เออ

เอียะ เอีย เอือะ เอือ อัวะ อัว ใอ ไอ

เอา อาว อุย โอย ออย เอย เอือย อวย

อิว เอ็ว เอว แอว เอียว ฤ ฤา ฦ ฦา

๑ ๒ ๓ ๔ ๕ ๖ ๗ ๘ ๙ ๐

ก ข ฃ ค ฅ ฆ ง

จ ฉ ช ซ ฌ ญ

ฎ ฏ ฐ ฑ ฒ ณ

ด ต ถ ท ธ น

บ ป ผ ฝ พ ฟ ภ ม

ย ร ล ว ศ ษ ส ห ฬ อ ฮ

อะ อา อ่ำ อิ อี อึ อื อุ อู เอะ เอ

แอะ แอ โอะ โอ เอาะ ออ เออะ เออ

เอียะ เอีย เอือะ เอือ อัวะ อัว ใอ ไอ

เอา อาว อุย โอย ออย เอย เอือย อวย

อิว เอ็ว เอว แอว เอียว ๆ ๅๅ ฯ ฯๅ

๑ ๒ ๓ ๔ ๕ ๖ ๗ ๘ ๙ ๐

ก ข ฃ ค ฅ ฆ ง

จ ฉ ช ซ ฌ ญ

ฎ ฏ ฐ ฑ ฒ ณ

ด ต ถ ท ธ น

บ ป ผ ฝ พ ฟ ภ ม

ย ร ด ว ศ ษ ส ห ฬ อ ฮ

อะ อา อำ อิ อี อึ อื อุ อู เอะ เอ

แอะ แอ โอะ โอ เอาะ ออ เออะ เออ

เอียะ เอีย เอือะ เอือ อัวะ อัว ใอ ไอ

เอา อาว อุย โอย ออย เอย เอือย อวย

อิว เอ็ว เอว แอว เอียว ฤ ฤๅ ฦ ฦๅ

๑ ๒ ๓ ๔ ๕ ๖ ๗ ๘ ๙ ๐

ก ข ฃ ค ฅ ฆ ง

จ ฉ ช ซ ฌ ญ

ฏ ฎ ฐ ฑ ฒ ณ

ด ต ถ ท ธ น

บ ป ผ ฝ พ ฟ ภ ม

ย ร ล ว ศ ษ ส ห ฬ อ ฮ

อะ อา อำ อิ อี อึ อื อุ อู เอะ เอ

แอะ แอ โอะ โอ เอาะ ออ เออะ เออ

เอียะ เอีย เอือะ เอือ อัวะ อัว ใอ ไอ

เอา อาว อุย โอย ออย เอย เอือย อวย

อิว เอ็ว เอว แอว เอียว ฤ ฤๅ ฦ ฦๅ

๑ ๒ ๓ ๔ ๕ ๖ ๗ ๘ ๙ ๐

---

ก ข ช ค ศ ฆ ง

จ ฉ ช ฌ ณ ญ

ฏ ฎ ฐ ฐ ฑ ฒ ณ

ด ต ถ ท ธ น

บ ป ผ ฝ พ ฟ ภ ม

ย ร ล ว ศ ษ ส ห ฬ อ ฮ

อะ อา อำ อิ อี อึ อื อุ อู เอะ เอ

แอะ แอ โอะ โอ เอาะ ออ เออะ เออ

เอียะ เอีย เอือะ เอือ อัวะ อัว ใอ ไอ

เอา อาว อุย โอย ออย เอย เอือย อวย

อิว เอ็ว เอว แอว เอียว ฤ ฤา ฦ ฦา

๑ ๒ ๓ ๔ ๕ ๖ ๗ ๘ ๙ ๐

The vowel signs of Indian and the Khmer form a different set to that of the consonants. They are written, as if as an afterthought, either before, after, above or below the consonants. It is so in present Thai writing. But in Ram Khamhaeng's scheme of writing it was otherwise. It is not out of place here to quote Dr. Cornelius B. Bradley, an American philologist, who says in his article "The oldest known writing in Siamese, the inscription of Phra Ram Khamhaeng of Sukhothai" *( The Journal of the Siam Society, vol. VI, part 1, p. 11, Bangkok 1909 )* thus:

"But the most original as well as the most interesting feature of his *( i.e. King Ram Khamhaeng's )* scheme of vowel-notation was his bringing of all the vowel signs into the written line along with the consonants, and so practically into the alphabet itself. Inclusion of the vowels in the alphabet was a master stroke of the Greek genius, when once for all it adapted oriental letters to the needs of a new world of life and thought. It is that alone, for example, which has made possible for all Western tongues the immense advantage of a perfectly fixed order of words in vocabularies, and lists. The lack of such absolute word-order is a difficulty and hindrance to scholarship more or less distinctly fell throughout the Eastern world, and everywhere for the same reason: — the vowels have no place in the alphabetical order. Prince Ram Khamhaeng, so far as we can learn, is the only man in all this interval who has come at all near to duplicating that old Grecian thought. But he did not carry his thought through to its logical conclusion. He did not give the vowels their place in the sequence of elements in the syllable, as he had given them in their place in the line.

Siamese scholars, unlike the Greek, were conning oriental scriptures. They thus kept ever alive the old tradition, and obscured the new. Very few years passed before the vowels which had been brought into the line were back in their old stations in the field. Thus it is that for Siamese of to-day, type that can be conveniently cast and set and dictionaries where words may be easily and certainly found, seem as unattainable as ever."

In 1917 A.D. King Vajiravudh revived this vowel scheme of notation of King Ram Khamhaeng as an experiment, but found no success. No doubt the old tradition of writing the vowel signs, like the original Indian and Khmer source, is still strong. With the exception of vowel notation as mentioned above, the writing of the Thai follows, fundamentally, King Ram Khamhaeng's writing up to the present day with certain modifications and additions due, of course, to the develop-ment of the writing.

As already mentioned, the Thai language is a tonal one where words of the same sound vary in meaning relevant to their tone. With the exception of the Thai of Thailand, all the written Thai words in different dialects, and also of the Shans and the Lao, have no written signs to mark the different tones of a word which sometimes varies from dialect to dialect. The Thai word for the verb to come (มา) or for horse (ม้า) and dog (หมา) is written as "mā" but pronounced in a different pitch. One cannot tell which "mā" is intended in writing. Only the context in the surrounding words will give a clue to it. But in Ram Khamhaeng's writing it is other-wise. He invented two tonal signs to mark the different tone in the word. In its development present Thai writing has four signs to mark the tones. Any person interested in the tonal system of the Thai language, can investigate the subject at some length by consulting the introduction to the Thai-English Dictionary by George B. McFarland, M.D. *(Bangkok, 1941; 2nd edition, Stanford, 1944).*

There are in the modern Thai or Siamese alphabet 44 consonants. Of these 16 of them are redundant, leaving in all 28 basic consonantal sounds. The redundant consonants are used chiefly in transliteration of Sanskrit and Pali words. In fact there are two consonants in this redundancy which are now obsolete. The arrangement of the letters of the alphabet follows the Sanskrit and Pali scheme, i.e. a division into six series related to the different places of contact in the production of consonantal sounds, and the language is written from left to right like English. Of the vowels there are 24 of them with 9 simple vowels and 12 diphthongs with corresponding relative long and short sounds. There are also 3 triphthongs, making in all 45 vowels both long and short. The final consonants of words or syllables are *k*, *t*, *p* or their corresponding nasal consonants and the two semi-vowels *y* and *w*. Such endings have unexplosive sounds. Words of foreign origin, especially Sanskrit and Pali, if ending in consonants other than *k*, *t*, *p* are usually pronounced like the above three consonants nevertheless. The writing and reading of words in a sentence are also from left to right, and there are no spaces or intervals between words. To a practised eye there is no great difficulty to be surmounted.

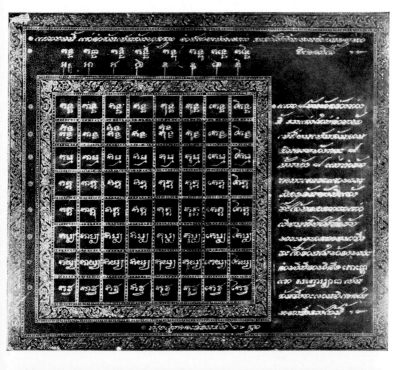

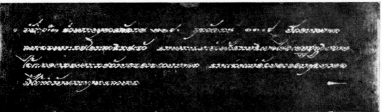

Cambodian scripts as used by the Siamese in "thai-ization" of Thai words, 1747 A.D.

# องก์ที่ ๒
## ตอนที่ ๑
### ฉาก: ดงอาร์เด็น

<u>เจ้านครผู้ถูกเนรเทศ ออก, พร้อมด้วยขุนนางอีกสองหรือสามนาย,
ซึ่งแต่งกายเป็นชาวป่า</u>

เจ้า   ดูก่อนสหายเราผู้เป็นน้องเรา
ถูกเคราะห์เคราะห์ว่าไปแล้ว,
เดี๋ยวเราอยู่คุ้มแล้วในดงดอน
ไม่เป็นสุขกว่าก่อนหรือฉันใด?
อันดงนี้มิภัยอปัจจกษณ
น้อยกว่าในปราสาทิกหรือฉันใด?
ในที่นี้ไม่มีทุกข์อันใดใด
นอกจากเปลี่ยนแปลงในฤดูกาล;
ยามลมหนาวพัดกลับมาอีก
ภาพทุกสิ่งมลายประหาร,
ถูกกัดเจ็บจริงหนาวสะท้าน,
กริ่มกมลจำนึงคำนึงใน:
"นี้มิใช่สอพลอยอกอดยศ:
มีอำนาจเตือนสติของเราให้
รู้สึกว่าเราเป็นผู้ใช่
ก็มิใช่อื่นแผกเผือกมนุษย์"
ความยากเข็ญนี้เหมือนว่าลืมตั้ง,
แม้ตัวคางคกน่าชังเป็นที่สุด
และมีพิษ, ใครเห็นก็หากทุด
ก็ยังมีพลอยผุดในหัวมัน: *

* ชาวยุโรปในสมัยที่เชกส์เปียร์ มีชีวิตอยู่นั้น เชื่อกันว่าในหัวคางคกมีพลอย
ชนิด ๑; ทั้งผู้รู้พากษ์มีพลอยชนิด ๑ ชัดคล้ายคางคก, หาได้ในประเทศอินเดียก็มี.

---

A translation of Shakespear's "*As You Like It*" in Thai
rhyming poem by King Vajiravudh, Rama VI *(A.D. 1880-1925)*
of Thailand.   A facimile of his running handwriting in Thai,

By using the invention of King Ram Khamhaeng's alphabet with each independent character like a Roman letter, the difficulty is alleviated to no less an extent in printing and typewriting. In 1892 Edwin McFarland, who was born in Thailand the son of an American missionary, brought with him after his return from America, the first Thai typewriter, which he had succeeded in making in that country. Owing to the array of the numerous characters of the Thai alphabet with its 44 consonants, 24 vowels and four tonal signs, he could not find any typewriter on the market that could accommodate all the Thai alphabet. At last he took a bold step by eliminating two Thai characters of the alphabet, i.e. ฃ.ฅ. which were rarely used in current writing. "Incidentally, these two letters gradually ceased to be used at all and to-day there are few who know that they ever existed". *(McFarland of Siam by Bertha Blount McFarland, Vintage Press, N.Y., 1958, p. 105)*

(For bibliography of the Thai language see *Bibliography of material about Thailand in Western languages, section language and literature* pp. 99-120, Chulalongkorn University, Bangkok, 1960).

❖   ❖   ❖

## Acknowledgement :

I am indebted to my friend Mr. Peter Bee of Chulalongkorn University, Bangkok, for his interest in the article. He has kindly read through it with certain important comments and corrected my English in many places for which I beg to express my deep thanks.

*The author*
*The Royal Institute, Bangkok*
**6th February, 1961**

# GENERAL SYSTEM OF PHONETIC TRANSCRIPTION OF THAI CHARACTERS INTO ROMAN

( As devised by the Royal Institute, Bangkok, 1954 )

## CONSONANTS

Note : — *English consonants except that*

*Initial* k p *and* t *are unaspirated as in French.*

*Final* k p *and* t *are unexplosive and unaspirated*

| | | |
|---|---|---|
| kh | = | k *aspirated* |
| ph | = | p *aspirated—not English* ph. |
| th | = | t *aspirated—not English* th. |
| čh | = | *hardened form of* ch *as the* cz *in Czech.* |
| ch | = | *always as in English* ' church '. |
| ng | = | *as in English* ' singer ', *never as in* ' linger '. |

| | Initial | Final |
|---|---|---|
| ก | k | k |
| ข ฃ ค ฅ ฆ | kh | k |
| ง | ng | ng |
| จ | čh | t |
| ฉ ช ฌ | ch | t |

— 32 —

|  | Initial | Final |
|---|---|---|
| ญ | y | n |
| ฅ ฎ ฑ *(when pronounced* d *)* | d | t |
| ฅ ฏ | t | t |
| ถ ฐ ฑ ฒ ธ ฌ | th | t |
| น ณ | n | n |
| บ | b | p |
| ป | p | p |
| ผ พ ภ | ph | p |
| ฝ ฟ | f | p |
| ม | m | m |
| ย | y | — |
| ร | r | n |
| ล ฬ | l | n |
| ว | w | — |
| ซ ทร ศ ษ ส | s | t |
| ห ฮ | h | — |

**Note:** — *In typing* čh *may be used for* ĉh

# VOWELS

**Note :** — *Italian Vowels except that*

æ = *sound of* ea *in English* ' *bear* '

ǫ = *sound of* aw *in English* ' *dawn* '

œ = *sound of* eu *in French* ' *peuple* '

uᶜ = *a sound more open than German* ü


| | |
|---|---|
| อะ อ อา | a |
| อ̊า | am |
| อิ อี | i |
| อึ อื | uᶜ |
| อุ อู | u |
| เอะ เอ เอ | e |
| แอะ แอ | æ |
| โอะ อ ( — ) โอ | o |
| เอาะ ออ | ǫ |
| เออะ เอ เออ — เอ̂ | œ ใ ฦ |
| เอียะ เอีย | iaใ ฦ |
| เอือะ เอือ | uᶜaใ |

| | |
|---|---|
| อัวะ อัว | ua |
| ใอ ไอ อัย ไอย อาย | ai |
| เอา อาว | ao |
| อุย | ui |
| โอย | oi |
| ออย | ǫi |
| เอย | œi |
| เอือย | u'ai |
| อวย | uai |
| อิว | iu |
| เอ็ว เอว | eo |
| แอว | æo |
| เอียว | ieo |
| ฤ *(when pronounced* ruᶜ *)* ฤๅ | ruᶜ |
| ฤ *(when pronounced* ri*)* | ri |
| ฤ *(when pronounced* roe*)* | rœ |
| ฦ ฦๅ | luᶜ |

**Note :—** *In typing* uᶜ *may be used for* u'
*and* ǫ *may be used for* ǫ

## Transcription of Words

Each syllable is to be separately transcribed in accordance with the characteristics of the Thai language.

### Examples

| | |
|---|---|
| กษัตริย์ | kasat |
| ประกาศ | prakat |
| ราชบุรี | Ratburi |

Th *hyphen is to be used where in the case of its omission the word may be read in another way.*

### Examples

| | |
|---|---|
| สอิง | sa-ing |
| ปากลัด | pak-lat |

### Marks of Quantity

*If found expedient, short vowels may be marked ( ˅ ).*